Lessons Learned Through Life In Christ Jesus

CLIFTON JONES, JR.

Lessons Learned Through Life In Christ Jesus
Copyright © 2022 by Clifton Jones, Jr.

ISBN
978-1-957895-49-9 (Paperback)
978-1-957895-48-2 (eBook)
978-1-957895-50-5 (Hardcover)

Dedication

This part of writing this book is real easy. I sincerely dedicate this book to my wife, Veronica Denise, who through much hurt and sorrow still waited for me. Honey I know it wasn't easy, but look what the end result brought! To my children who have done without entirely too long, but praise God that He is faithful. And to all of my brothers and sisters, family and friends who continue to stay strong in the struggle. Hold on, your change is on the way. So don't wait fill the Battle's over, shout in victory now! God Bless & I love you all.

Table of Contents

Acknowledgments 1

Prelude 3

Introduction 7

Section One Praying / Seed 9

Lesson 1 Ground breaking................................11

Lesson 2 Talk to me!......................................17

Lesson 3 Did I hear right?................................21

Lesson 4 If you say so 25

Section Two Preparation / Time 29

Lesson 5 Just Wait!...31

Lesson 6 In the meantime 35

Lesson 7 Signs of Progress.............................39

Lesson 8 Got Room?.......................................45

Section Three Provision / Harvest 51

Lesson 9 Prep Time 53

Lesson 10 Let it Flow 59

Lesson 11 Hold the load 65

Lesson 12 Over and Over Again......................69

Scriptural Reference 73

Appendix 75

Acknowledgments

I would like to thank my Dear GOD fearing cousins Douglas and Bernadette Harrell for their loving support through it all. To people like Dr. Creflo & Taffi Dollar, Kenneth & Gloria Copeland, Joyce Meyers, Bishop T.D. Jakes, the late Kenneth Hagan, Sr. and Kenneth Hagin, Jr., Dr. Leroy Thompson, Mark Hagins, Oral Roberts, and Billy Graham. Thanks for all the incredible teachings! Finally but in no way the least, my mother and father Clifton and Josie Jones. I'll see you when I get there! Oh and I didn't forget my little brother, Gerrod Thomas, keep flowin' in Him!

Prelude

Everything has to have a purpose. A point of understanding to be reached. A method to the ordered madness of our modern day society. Something to give us stability and focus.

Something that holds us in check as individuals. Something to keep us all anchored within this sea of constant upheaval. A candle, if you will, of order that chases away the shadows of discontentment and chaotic darkness.

Usually your average individual would seek solace in family, friends, activities or careers. This only stages itself as a bandage over a cancer. It won't do the job needed. And whether or not one seeks stability in any of the previous mentioned ways, one's purpose even through these ways though earnestly hoped and looked for can not be formed in the mere activities and unions that life seems to offer.

It's as if life says, "Be all you can be" without illustrating, "how do I do it." I have always been made aware of the resounding cry of humanity to either find themselves, be true to themselves, or somehow transform themselves into this social being who in theory would be complete. I've not been successful.

Now by using these, a persons purpose is supposedly tied somehow into it all. With the assumption that if I find myself, I'll locate my purpose. If I be true to myself, I'll then embrace my purpose. Then, as I learn whatever my purpose is, assuming I can find a way to transform myself, then my purpose can be achieved.

Well though I being one who has searched, been honest, and tried transforming in every earthly way, it just didn't get me anywhere.

Now before you allow yourself to think that I'm finding fault with the hundreds of self–help books, motivational tapes and what I like to call "Get in touch with yourself "seminars, in all truth I'm only putting in my proverbial "two cents worth."

Man has to do something. What I mean is humanity at some point in time has to come to a crossroad of decision and not only ask, but ultimately figure out what am I going to do with me, myself and I.

Whatever you choose, one must apply what one learns within their quest for success. Whether it's through social units, activities, or religion. Lessons must be learned and practiced. I personally chose the religions route for success and thus far it has proved itself more than sufficient. Yes, I'm a Christian.

No I'm not any of the great men or women who are well known for their tremendous efforts in the gospel, and I'm sorry but I don't have any major accolades or Theological titles behind my name. I'm just a man who loves God and wants to share what He has given me with anyone who would listen. I hope you learn as well. God Bless.

Introduction

In the Bible, Ecclesiastes chapter three verse one makes a fundamental statement along with Mark chapter four verses twenty six thru twenty nine which basically says that in the former, there is a season or time for every thing. And in the latter, it explains the process of seed, time, and harvest or if you will prayer, preparation, and provision.

Through these scriptures God has shown me an interesting yet simple cycle to follow when I'm in need of help, heeling, or deliverance. This book will illustrate this process in the form of Twelve chapters separated by three sections to show this pattern of success. Scripture reference throughout this book can be found in the Appendix.

Now remember anything that is learned must be applied in a consistent manner in order for true success. To try this pattern once or twice without review of this book frequently would be the equivalent of buying a new car, filling the tank on a couple occasions, then refusing to buy gas anymore. You're just not going to get anywhere real fast, So let's begin.

Section One
Praying / Seed

There is a time for everything, and a season for every activity under Heaven.

Ecclesiastes 3:1 N.I.V.

... "this is what the Kingdom of God is like. A man scatters seed on the ground. Night and Day, whether he sleeps or gets up, the seed sprouts and grows, though he does not know how. All by itself the soil produces grain — first the stalk, then the head, then the full kernel in the head. As soon as the grain is ripe, he puts the sickle to it, because the harvest has come.

Mark 4:26– 29 N.I.V.

Lesson 1
Ground breaking

I grew up in a small rural town in Central Louisiana in and at a time when things changed slowly. But that was kind of expected when one is born in the 60's, grew through child hood and adolescence in the 70's and came of age, in a manner of speaking , in the 80's. One of the true attributes about living in what we affectionately called the country, was that we always had time to observe the world around us.

Since there wasn't a lot of major activities to get involved in, focusing ones attention on anything that didn't involve some sort of technical wizardry wasn't uncommon. Especially when one wanted to play a video game he would actually suffer through the toil of having to walk or ride a bicycle to the local game room. Far be it from the mind of any parent to cause such a strenuous activity for children today making them leave the comfort for their home entertainment, slash video game center to find out that life can still be interesting and exciting without a Game boy or "X" Box. Let me get to my point.

My dad grew up on a farm, and even though we lived in the heart of town, people in the neighborhood still raised small amounts of livestock, and mostly everybody had their very own garden. And of course it was no different with us.

I remember my father showing me, at the age of seven, how to prepare a garden with all the basic tools required for such a task. With a shovel, hoe and garden rake we begin the laborious task of getting the ground manageable, or as we put it "working the land."

Now in all honesty, I was more interested in chasing butterflies and what we called mosquito hawks then actually trying to accomplish anything regarding gardening! But one rule was instilled upon me and that was, you can't plant a seed until the ground is ready. This same rule would help change my life completely. You see this is a spiritual truth that must be understood before any form of substantial success can be achieved. The Bible teaches us that ground— breaking is essential in ones hope to travel from a spiritual point A to B.

Now in reference to mankind, we as spirit beings are frequently compared to as the ground that must be prepared for use. More specifically the heart of man is the chosen area mandated for cultivation. In the books of Jeremiah and Hosea we hear word of having the heart of man made ready by breaking up the fallowed ground of the heart. (1) We see a clearer picture of this in Psalms 51 when David tells us that, "The sacrifices of God are a broken spirit, a broken and contrite heart, the Lord will not despise. But how does one reach or come to such levels?

In most cases located throughout the Bible this is brought about by learning the soul—stirring hand clapping and of course heart piercing word of God that can separate bone from marrow and soul from spirit. This can usually bring about two emotional states. Radiant Joy or heart wrenching sorrow.

Both to be used to bring the individual to the point of asking the aged long question,

"What must I do to be saved?" I have always been amazed as to how the crowd reacted after the now all too famous speech on the Day of Pentecost that Peter gave as explanation for their then strange actions. (2)

We must remember that not Peter nor even the words by themselves moved the people but the power of God in the Holy Spirit that gave those words the ability to stir emotions give hope and wound hearts in accordance to God's will. And through this great movement of the Spirit lives are changed because the spiritual heart of man which was beforehand hard and callus ridden, has now because of the spoken word of God in faith, brought about a change of mind and/or thinking. And this change of heart is in essence the point of having the ground of the heart made ready for receiving seed.

Now we must understand that if we are the ground so— to— speak, then the word that we receive is the seed that is planted in our hearts! Now let's take it a bit further. Before we close this chapter, there are some very interesting points we need to see that Jesus points out to us in the parable of the sower. We see in this parable that there are basically four stages of ground that we as Christians should he familiar with. They are:

1. Rough well trodden ground that's completely un— prepared for anything.
2. Ground where soil and rocks are mixed.
3. Ground that has not been weeded out.
4. Well tilled soil that has been thoroughly cultivated. (3)

Each one of these examples of different types of ground are shown in the scripture to represent a heart that cannot receive a word due to failure to reach the person. A heart that receives a word, but because does not hold up against the strain of daily pressures. Yet another heart that has ground that although has been tilled was not thoroughly weeded and the word is then compromised due to the many extras of life that represents weeds. And finally a heart that has been well plowed prepared and cleansed with the word and thereby brings forth excellent results.

Now each example can be seen as a different person at a time in their life when the word is needed, for the scripture does remind us that true love , joy, and peace are promised to all who would be willing to receive the free gift of salvation. For this is promised to all the Lord our God will call.

But it also could be different stages in one persons life as God prepares or molds a person to His perfect will for their lives. With each level experienced through the hurts of rejections and loneliness having our hearts trodden over by an uncaring world leaving us easy prey for the enemy. Yet learning to submit to the will of God will, with the hope and zeal that comes from hearing the word of deliverance, inspires us to reach for great heights, but because of a lack of spiritual knowledge by studying, meditating, and prayer would have brought stability, not the lack of, when pressures of life caused us to let the word die. But God is faithful, and we hear Him lovingly calling us, yet this time because of peer pressures, bad company and the like we don't reach full potential. Finally we start all over again wizened by our experience, trials and errors now come forth as receives of the word that produces great gain. Now only the individual knows where or what level they are on with God. My point is that if you do recognize yourself in any of the earlier stages mentioned and really want to reach that fourth level, I would suggest you pray this prayer with me.

- Father God, I come to you in the spirit of meekness and with thanksgiving. Father I have come to recognize that my heart is unprepared to receive all the wonderful benefits that You have promised according to your word. Therefore Father I humbly ask you even in accordance to your word, to give me a clean, recreated heart and renew within me a right, steadfast spirit that I may whole heartedly receive, maintain, and bring forth the fullness of all you would have me to do, Jesus' name, Amen.

Now let's meditate on lesson number one: "Always remember that your ground / heart must be prepared / broken to receive the word / seed."

- The Appendix has other prayers set in order of the lesson.

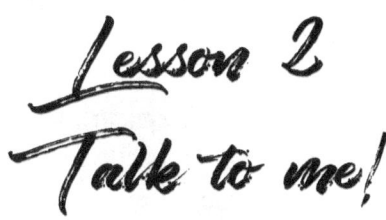

Lesson 2
Talk to me!

Problem solving— the process of finding a solution to whatever problem that one is faced with. Now the trouble starts when the problem just does not seem to have an applicable solution. So then what?

Many Christians can agree upon the fact that either at one point or another within their spiritual walk, they've faced problems that seem to be over— whelming. And aside from coming to the point of wanting to pull your hair out trying to cope with the situation, the problems always seem to have a greater yet un— detected motive. Drawing us closer to God.

God wants to solve all our problems, heal all our hurts and meet all our needs. Why, because it's His very nature to save, protect, provide, prepare and comfort us concerning whatever the world and the devil can throw at us. Remember prayers are word seeds.(1)

Now the question that arises is why doesn't God, who can do anything, simply eliminate the problems. Well one of the reasons is that God uses our problems to mold us into the true vessels of honor that He desires us to be.

Secondly there's an interesting story that answers this question from a rarely known or understood view. In the

Book of Judges in chapters two and tree, ending in verse four of chapter three.

It basically gives insight by explaining that God allowed the warning nations that opposed the Hebrews to remain in the promised land to be used as rods of affliction thereby causing them to always seek Him during times of need. You see God knows that people in general have a tendency to become overly confident in their own ability. Thus causing arrogance and pride to blindfold us to the treachery of the enemy that leads us to a point of spiritual isolation that can cause severe and costly damage to the person.

Thank God for His loving ability to use such unsettling situations even today in our lives to bring about a bond of trust and confidence in Him. This is why in developing a personal relationship with God we learn to depend on the mercies of our Lord and Savior Jesus, knowing that when a problem arises on matter how large or devastating we can call on God in prayer and yes expect an answer. For by faith we know He hears us and since we know He hears us we have confidence that He will grant us the petition that we request according to His will. Now what I've come to realize is that we pray sincerely in most cases but not always according to His will. And God's will is recording. It's the Bible itself Words are seeds.

When we pray in accordance to the word of God concerning our situations we can expect greater results. Why, because God is moved by faith in His Word. The Bible says that without faith it is impossible to please Him, for we must believe that He is in truth God and therefore a rewarder of those who diligently, consistently, and purposefully seek Him. (2)

And we have to have that same confidence and trust in God's word as we have in God

himself. God says He watches over His word to perform it or bring it to pass. (Make it a reality). (4) He also tells us that His word goes out, (to accomplished) but will indeed accomplish and achieve the purpose for which I sent it. (5) God's word is just as important and carries as much authority as His name. (6) Now with all this in mind we need to line up our words in prayer with whatever God's word says about our problem. It's that simple.

We need to understand that God speaks to us through and by His word. He won't do anything that does not line up with His word. And He is accountable to His word. So God will provide solutions, answers and remedies by His word.

We as Christians need to become more familiar with God's word. Jesus said, "that the spirit gives life; the flesh counts for nothing. The words I have spoken to you are Spirit and they are life. (7) So while we are facing a problem that seems to be more than we can handle, and we pray frantically crying out to God to "Talk to me" remember He's speaking in volumes about your problem in His word. So let us read and meditate upon what He says about our situations and apply that word in prayer that we've received from God. Remember to pray what He says and you've already won half the battle.

Now let's meditate on lesson number 2. God's word speaks volumes to us concerning all our situations and we will have victory when we speak what God tells us through His word. Remember God talks to us! And He will talk to you.

Lesson 3
Did I hear right?

Speak Lord, for thy servant is listening. These were the words that the young boy named Samuel was told to say by Eli the priest if he again heard the voice of someone calling him in the night.

This story is recorded in the book of r Samuel chapter three, and through this chapter and event, we will learn another point of interest regarding what happens after speaking to God, and ultimately hearing from God, one must now press through the mental and emotional maze that constantly raises the question, "Did I hear right?"

Many times we pray and receive a word from God yet due to certain truths that arise we even wonder have we actually heard from God or are we imagining things by seeing more into the word than what is actually there.

One of the problems that causes this is a lack of personal experience dealing with the word. For instance scripture says in 15` Samuel 3:1, "The boy Samuel ministered before the Lord under Eli. In those days the word of the Lord was rare; there were not many visions.

In chapter one we learned that one of the reasons the word does not mature fully in ones heart is due to the constant interruptions that the world seems to afflict upon the mind of the Christian becoming a major distraction. These continual distractions can cause our senses to become dull and this even occurs in a spiritual aspect as well. If I'm always being bombarded by the cares of this world; family matters, job, home responsibilities mixed in with personal problems it can be quite difficult to distinguish whom I'm hearing from.

If a person is not used to hearing from God on a regular basis, usually due to a lack of spiritual closeness, one can miss the message that God is giving them. Like in Samuel's day, the word of the Lord can be rare in the lives of many Christians because of a failure to be made and remain aware of how God speaks to us.

Now notice that in verse one the Bible tells us that the boy Samuel ministered before the Lord. This means that Samuel served God. By being available to God, becoming a true worshiper of God. True worshipers please God. Not with our words only, but with our actions coinciding with words we profess. When our walk in Christ Jesus is shown in our everyday activities to the glory of His name, then we please God. We minister before God in a procession of faith, hope, and love. Believing God's word unconditionally, trusting God without wavering, and loving God wholeheartedly. God measures your love, faith and hope in Him by your actions or how you minister to the needs of others.

I have come to learn that even though God will use visions to speak to his people, it is through His word that He most frequently speaks. Why, because the word is proven, tried and true, and will last forever. His Word stands unaided and supported by the undeniable true that God is not a man that He should lie nor the son of man that He should repent or change His mine.(1)

His Word is tangible, something we can hold on to. The book of Hebrews 11:3 says that by faith we understand that the universe was formed by God's word...

This is a truth that is evident in all that is around us. And it was all made by the spoken word of God. As you continue to trust God and walk in willingness to serve Him and being obedient to His will, you'll find that God will speak to you and His word will seemingly jump off the pages and into your heart being seed sown to bring victory and deliverance regarding whatever you're faced with.

In verse 21 of 1st Samuel three scripture says, The Lord continued to appear at Shiloh, and there He revealed himself to Samuel through His word. And Samuel's word came to all Israel. Remember as you grow closer to God he will reveal Himself to you through His Word, and as you are made aware of His word, His word then becomes your word to apply to your problem. Now in our next chapter we'll talk a little more about applying what He says in faith.

Now let's meditate on lesson number 3. We can be made confident that as we continue to worship God and grow closer to Him, we will be able to distinguish His Word to us from everything else.

Lesson 4
If you say so

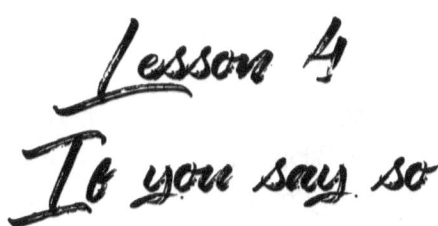

In the book of John in the 6th Chapter within verses 63 and 64 we see Jesus making a statement in truth that reveals the lesson of this chapter. A lesson that is so often seen throughout the Bible yet overlooked by many.

We are about to address within this chapter how sometimes when God gives an answer to our problem through instruction, though the Word seems awkward regarding it's answer, we due to this strangeness are unsure and do not follow the instructions and therefore miss the mark of having our prayer answered.

Yes, sometimes what God instructs seems to be somewhat of a paradox. Yet we can not be hampered by our need to always try to rationalize Gods' instructions which is based upon His infinite wisdom.

In John 6:63– 64 Jesus said, "The Spirit gives life, the flesh counts for nothing. The words that I have spoken to you are spirit, and they are life. Yet there are some of you who do not believe. For Jesus had known from the beginning which of them did not believe and who would betray Him." Don't allow your thinking to block your blessing.

God spoke through Isaiah the prophet telling us that His thoughts are not our thoughts neither are His ways like our ways. (I) So we have to realize that what we may deem strange, God considers normal.

Imagine, if you will, what would have happened if many of the people of the Bible would not have taken God at His word and obediently followed His instructions. Noah not ever seeing rain before could have built the Ark with pine or cypress, not Gopher wood as God instructed, or not been obedient and built the Ark at all for that matter. What if Naaman would have refused to listen to the urging of one of his servants to follow the instructions giving to him by Elisha the prophet necessary for his healing. What if the Ten lepers would have not followed Jesus' instruction to go show themselves to the priest. "Too much thinking on our part can open the door to doubt and close the door to deliverance."

Let us stop allowing the fear of the unknown or inability to understand everything like we deem necessary to hinder us of our victories that God wants us to have.

If we say we love Him yet do not do the things He says, then our love is counterfeit.(2) When Jesus made this statement we know he was referring to being willing and obedient. Yet is it not with the same reasoning that we should be just as willing and obedient to following the instructions He gives concerning our healing, deliverance, or victory that we so anxiously desire? Of course it is!

Let's stop all of the second guessing and afterthoughts concerning God's answers for our situation. Remember it is God who gives seed to the sower, so He knows what type of seed is necessary to bring about the right crop. Trust God.

Now let's meditate on lesson number 4. Even though at times God's answers may seem to be paradoxical, follow

His instruction to the letter for in doing so, you will reap a harvest of victory, success, and deliverance in whatever you need. So let's believe God whole heartedly and take Him at His word for in doing so we are opening up the gates to all that God promises.

Section Two
Preparation / Time

I waited patiently for the Lord; He turned to me and heard my cry.

Psalms 40:1 NIV

Wait for the Lord; be strong and take heart and wait for the Lord.

Psalms 27:14 NIV

How long, O Lord? Will you forget me forever? How long will you hide your face from me? How long must I wrestle with my thoughts and everyday have sorrow in my heart?

Psalms 13:1– 2 NIV

Let us not become weary in doing good, for at the proper time we will reap a harvest if we do not give up.

Galatians 6:9 NIV

Lesson 5
Just Wait!

When I was a child growing up in the rural south, I vividly recall going to church services with my parents every Sunday. And I can recall listening to the choir sing about the man in the Bible who had to wait on the Lord.

That was Job. And there was one verse that always stood out in my mind. It said, "He may not come when you want Him, but He's always on time." And then as if it were a rehearsed theme a deacon would read the scripture in Psalms where David said for us to wait upon the Lord and be of good courage.

Waiting has not always been one of my strong points to say the least. But the truth of the matter is that time does bring about a change. Yet not without learning the importance of patience.

In this chapter we're going to focus on the fact that God moves according to His set time and we as His children must learn the art of waiting on the Lord! The word of God plays a major role in our stability. We've previously discussed in section one the process on preparing to receive a word from God and move upon that word in faithfulness, and obedience according to the instructions God gives us to follow.

Now in short, a good definition for the meaning of faith is believing that the Word or God is absolutely true. Faith is a key factor needed when establishing a relationship with God. Faith moves God. But faith when coupled with patience is vital when one is expecting results from God.

I cannot express this one statement enough "God moves when He wants to." We can cry, rant, rave, shout, run around in circles, and even fast day in and day out. We must accept the truth that our God is Sovereign, and His choices are sovereign as well. His timing for deliverance is already set for each and every one of us.

Now what anchors us in faith, giving us the ability to wait, is the same word of instruction that we received from God. Let me explain it like this. If you can pray, and then because of your relationship with God, be made aware that He is speaking to you through the word, and ultimately receive a word of deliverance from the Lord concerning your situation, then you can use those same scriptures you used to build your faith to be a foundation for you to wait on.

When we take the word and use it as a tool to remind us of the steadfastness of God in any situation, we'll begin to develop a confidence in the way God does things. We can all look back into our past and glance at problems that we thought were going to surely bring us to the breaking point, yet God brought us threw.

We need to learn from one of the psalmist Asaph who wrote in the 77th Psalm that, "I will remember the deeds of the Lord; yes, I will remember your miracles of long ago. I will meditate on all your works and consider all your mighty deeds." In verses 11 and 12 we see that it is very important to remind ourselves of just how wonderful, loving, and trustworthy our God really is.

In chapter one of this book, I told you how my Dad taught me about gardening. Well after the ground was made ready, we would dig holes to drop the seeds in, then cover them up again. I remember running back and forth every few hour for the first couple of days and then becoming discouraged and about to loose interest completely in the whole project. Then my Dad explained to me that everything worth having is worth waiting for, and good things come to those who wait.

This is so true regarding Gods' blessings for us. We know that God is a good God, and everything He does is good. (1) The word tells us that every good and perfect gift comes from God. (2) When we wait on the Lord we show that we trust Him completely. Isaiah 40:31 says, but those that hope in the Lord will renew their strength. They will soar on wings like eagles; they will run and not grow weary, they will walk and not be faint.

When we look to God's Word for support while we wait, God will strengthen us and give us the power to maintain until our change or deliverance comes.

Like Job said in the 14th chapter of the book of Job 14th verse; " If a man dies, will he live again? Through all the days of my appointed time will I wait until my change comes." Sometimes it may seem like it's taking forever, but be assure, its' not. For those of us in Christ Jesus will see our change come if we just hold on.

So let's trust God in faith and search out His word seeing how he never fails. Think about all the Lordships that He's already brought you through. And remember that trouble does not last always because like every other problem you've faced, it too will pass. Just pray and wait!

Now let's meditate on lesson number 5. Let us use the Word of God and the memories of what God has previously brought us through as an anchor to hold us firm in faith until our change or victory comes to pass. God will not forget!

Lesson 6
In the meantime

So what do we do while waiting for our change to come? I have learned that this question is sometimes answered in the wrong way. Let me explain.

Many times while we as Christians are waiting for God we search for a way to pass the time away. Like reading magazines in the lobby of a salon or barbershop, we try to find things to do that will occupy our time. Actually what we're doing is trying to flood our minds with other thoughts in order not to focus on our problems.

The problem that arises from this form of thinking is that it only gives a very temporary and limited amount of relief. We've all done this at one point or another in our lives to help cope with our issues we face.

We do this mostly because we want to avoid worrying. And we know that worrying over matters that we've given to God in prayer indicates a form of a lack of faith. Knowing we can only please and move God by faith. So we don't want to be found lacking in faith therefore we will do whatever it takes to keep our minds from thinking about what God will do, or when will He move, or has He moved yet?

Now this type of avoidance can lead us into escapism and that can become real dangerous to the Christian. Know that God does not want you to worry but He doesn't want you to harm yourself by not dealing with your feelings and thoughts concerning the matter.

As a matter of fact, God wants to get directly involved with you to help you deal with the waiting process. How? Through the working of the word we learn to not focus on the problem but focus on the solution and the victory it brings.

When God gives us that word of wisdom that once applied will bring about victory, we then need to take hold of that word and build on it and literally begin to think positive thoughts about the situation. In other words, start seeing something!

Now I don't mean becoming delusional or anything of the sort. I mean begin to use your renewed mind to focus on the believed and hoped for relief that you are trusting God for.

My fellow Christians we have got to become men and women of vision! When we pray about a problem the scripture tells us in St. Mark 11:24 that we must believe that we have already received our results.

We have to use our God given imagination to see ourselves healed. To see ourselves out of debt. To see ourselves delivered and victory bound! God spoke to the prophet Jeremiah in the book of Jeremiah chapter 1, verse 11 and 12 asking him what did he see? When Jeremiah responded in faith about what he saw to God, God's response was that he saw correctly, and that He, God was watching over His word to perform it. Now this is what God is saying to us. When we ask for help, He sends His word to us to heal, encourage, enlighten, deliver, give wisdom, impute knowledge and bring about the required and asked for victory! His word is Spirit and is life! His word inspires and gives hope. And that same word can be seen if you allow yourself to think upon what He has said.

For instance, if you are sick and you have prayed to God for help and He leads you to stand on His word in 1st Peter 2:24 telling you that by Jesus's wounds you are already healed, then you need to imagine yourself healed! See yourself whole and healthy. And that what you've imagined, due to your thoughts will give you a new confidence to speak that what you see. And once you start to believe what you think and then speak what you've believed, then you will find yourself walking in the Spirit of faith. (1)

When the scripture says we walk by faith and not by sight. (2) It means that we do not limit ourselves to what is physically or presently seen, for those things are subject to change.

We walking by the "spiritual sights" that are physically unseen at the present time. That what we see is built upon the word that God has given us and like our fore— father Abraham we are not shaken or made to stagger at the promises that God has given through His word, but are indeed strengthened by it. Now truly believing God who gives life to the dead and calls the things that are not as though they were. (3)

With the spirit— filled word of God acting on our behalf, coming out of our months with an assurance and confidence that is being driven forward by the proven power of the word of God, we will not only find ourselves no longer worrying about the problem, but meditating on the word that we now visualize coming to pass in our lives.

Now let's meditate on lesson number 5. While waiting for our change to come, let's not allow ourselves to worry, but concentrate on what God has said about our problem and allow ourselves to see our deliverance come to pass by using our imaginations in a positive way.

Lesson 7
Signs of Progress

Now that we have learned to wait for our change to come in a positive way we can now expect to see the beginnings of results regarding our situation. These beginnings are what I call signs of progress.

Now the key to discovering these signs revolves around knowing what to look for. Scripture says God's word does not go out, and come back void, but will accomplish what it's sent out to do. We must keep in mind that a process is at work and with every process there will be signs of change or progress.

Let's use healing for an example. If I've been praying for a healing in my body, I after receiving a word from God concerning; instructing, or proclaiming my healing, must allow this word to heal my mind first. Why, because we have to have a mind set for healing in order to be completely healed. Romans 12:2 says, "Do not conform any longer to the pattern of this world, but be transformed by the renewing of your mind. Then you will be able to test and approve what God's will is — His good, pleasing and perfect will."

You can't be healed if your mind has not been conditioned by the word to accept the truth that God wants you to be healthy and whole in all areas of your life. 3rd John 1:2 let us know that we should be healthy physically, mentally, emotionally, socially, and financially as well as spiritually. This is God's desire for us all.

There as wonderful point made concerning this topic in Psalm 34 verses 4 thru 6 which reads according to the New International Version as follows: "I sought the Lord and He answered me He delivered me from all my fears. Those who look to Him are radiant; their faces are never covered with shame. This poor man called and the Lord heard Him; He delivered or saved him out of all his troubles."

In verse 4 the psalmist states that he sought the Lord and the Lord answered. He was first delivered from all his fears. Our fears are holding our hopes hostage and can only be freed by the word of God. For God did not give us a spirit of fear, but a spirit of power, love, and a sound mind!(1)

We receive the power of God by faith in that same Word that was preached to us that God used to prick our hearts and set us on the path of salvation in Christ Jesus. Once we accepted Jesus as Lord and Savior of our lives, the Holy Spirit moved in and took up residence in our spirit. Or as I like to say, the seed of faith was then planted in the fallowed ground of the heart and has taken root.

The love of God is shown forth in us as we continued to pray, study, and fellowship as the Lord has instructed us in His word. But the sound mind is developed as we take the word of God and constantly meditate on it as we reinforce our faith daily in it. This same sound mind is the mind that has been renewed by the Word. This same sound mind is the mind that has been delivered from all fears! How, through the Holy Spirit– filled word of faith that is ever increasing day by day in the believer. And once this fear is hammered out of the mind by the sufficiency of His word, the believer is now enabled to notice the changes as they appear even first in his thinking.

You see once you start to think different about a thing, you begin to look at it in a whole new light. You begin to speak differently about it, because of your new outlook concerning the situation. Remember you're now using the word to build a foundation that now allows you to imagine yourself delivered.

How you speak, think, and see yourself concerning your situation are all signs of progress stemmed from the renewed mind that has been made sound by the word that you received in faith even in response to your situation. Once you start to recognize such changes, your confidence will increase even more letting you know that your blessing is on the way.

If we never begin to recognize change concerning the way we view the problem, this is a sign that we have not fully allowed our thought process to be changed from a *worldly* format to a *word-ly* format. This let's us know we need to spend more time in the word and in prayer and even consult God in regards to fasting if needed. Now the fast will not in itself or by itself move God. We know that faith moves God. But when our faith is weak in a certain area, or concerning a certain problem, your fast is enhancing your ability to walk in faith.

God wants to save us out of all our troubles. But we must allow Him to free our minds first. The Bible tells us that Israel was in Egypt for four hundred years held in bondage and being contaminated by the effects of the ways of life of the Egyptians. The journey from Egypt to Canaan should have took no more than a few weeks tops. Yet instead it took 40 years and the lost of an entire generation before they could enter in. (2) Why so long? Simply put, it only took a few weeks to get Israel out of Egypt, but it took 40 years to get Egypt and her sinful ways out of Israel. Remember the way you think can reveal a whole lot.

Now lets' meditate on lesson number 7. As you change the way you think thru the power of the word of God, you will be able to recognize a change in your outlook and speech concerning your problem, which represent signs of progress.

Lesson 8
Got Room?

There have been several points of importance that we have addressed in this section and in this chapter we will look at a very interesting and essential part that bridges the gap between seed, time and harvest. Walking out in faith what God has said to you.

We do this as an act of willingness and obedience to what God has instructed us to do. We have to remember that when God makes a promise, He will bring it to pass. We activate our faith in what God has said by what we do. In other words if I have been praying for a financial blessing that will enable me to purchase a car, then I'm going to begin looking for that car via the local car lots, newspaper, television commercials, or even the inter net.

Now this may sound a bit farfetched but let me give you two biblical examples of acts of faith as people made preparations to receive the blessings that they were believing God for. The first story is found in the book of 2"" Kings chapter 4 verses 1 thru 7. It tells of a woman who was a widow of a man who was of the company of the prophets, who after the death of her husband was found in need of major financial help. So much to the point that the creditors of her day were threatening to enslave her sons in order that the debt would be compensated.

So she ran to the man of God, the prophet Elisha and voiced her dilemma. After hearing her out, Elisha asked how could he help her, and what do you have in your house. She explained that she had nothing left at all except a little oil. Elisha instructed her to go to her neighbors and borrow all of the empty jars she could find, not just a few, but as many as she could get. She was to go inside her house, she and her sons with all the empty jars and close themselves up in the house. Then begin to pour oil into the empty jars and as one got full, set it to the side and continue to pour into another. Once all the jars had been filled from the small amount that she began with, the oil stopped. Then on returning to Elisha he told her to go and sell the oil and pay her creditors and live off the remaining amount made from the oil.

Now there are three points to consider that are essential in this story. (1) The widow had a problem that she could not solve and she sought help from the prophet. When we are faced with unsurmountable problems we seek God in prayer. (2) The prophet Elisha gave instruction that would bring about a solution. God will give us a word of faith to be acted upon to bring about our needed change. (3) Due to the willingness and the obedience of the widow to act in faith and follow the instructions of the prophet not only was her problem solved but the remedy was even greater than the problem presented. When we trust in God's word of instruction and act out in faith making preparations to receive that which we've prayed for, we can surely look forward to a greater increased solution that brings about a deliverance not just an answer.

What I mean by this is that God just doesn't want to solve or answer your problem, but He wants to bless you in a way that will bring about complete victory over the matter. He doesn't just want to pay your overdue bills but set you free from debt!

Notice that not only did God answer her request, but He also blessed above her assumed prayer. God knew that she needed a financial blessing big enough to place her into a point of financial security. Why did God do this? Because His mercy does endure forever and His love for us is uncomprehensible.

In Ephesians 3:20 it tells us that God will do exceeding abundantly above all that we could ask or think according to the power that works in us. This tells us that God wants his people empowered to prosper. Through her faith, she placed herself in a position to receive the most from God. Remember, the prophet told her not to get a few jars signifying that God wanted to pour out to her greatly. Enough to exceed her present request yet sufficient to meet her unseen needs. The second example is found in John 2:1– 11.

Jesus was at a wedding banquet and a need for more wine arose. Mary, the mother of Jesus, told Jesus that the host had run out of wine. The request was made concerning the problem to the problem solver. Mary in faith told the servants to do whatever He says.

Jesus then gave instruction to take the water jars, which were used for ceremonial washing, and fill them up with water. So the servants filled the jars to the brim in obedience. Jesus then told them to draw some out and take it to the master of the banquet.

After the request was made concerning what was needed in faith, a word of instruction was given. In willingness and obedience, to the prompting of Mary, the servants filled the jars to the brim with water and brought some to the master or the host.

When the water which had been turned into wine was tasted by the host, he signaled to have a word with the bridegroom, and said that most people would have brought out the good wine first, (not knowing where what he was now drinking came from), but he had saved the best for last. Once again God did above and beyond what was requested by not just making wine, but supplying them with wine of the utmost premium value.

The servants could have easily went and got some serving pitchers which would have probably been much more convenient rather than wrestling with the large cumbersome water jars which held up to twenty or thirty gallons of water when full.

But due to the obedience and willingness that was shown forth in their act of faith, not only was wine made but the best was now in supply in great quantity.

Both of these examples have many comparisons. But the outstanding one we want to focus on is that in both cases, the widow and the wedding servants, made room for their miracles. They made preparations for their coming provision. So let's step out in faith, and make sure we've got room, lots of room for our blessing.

Now let's meditate on lesson number 8. Let's dedicate ourselves to prepare for the exceeding abundantly above what we ask or think blessing that God has in store for us.

Section Three
Provision / Harvest

For the Lord our God is the one who goes with you to fight for you against you enemies to give you victory.

Deuteronomy 20:4 NIV

For those who sow in tears will reap with songs of joy. He who goes out weeping caring seed to sow will return with songs of joy.

Psalms 126:5 – 6 NIV

But blessed is the man who trusts in the Lord, whose confidence is in Him. He will be like a tree planted by the water that sends out it's roots by the stream. It does not fear when heat comes; its leaves are always green. It has no worries in a year of drought and never fails to bear fruit.

Jeremiah 17:7 – 8 NIV

We do not want you to become lazy, but to imitate those who through faith and patience inherit what has been promised.

Hebrews 6:12 NIV

Lesson 9
Prep Time

In our last chapter, we discussed the importance of walking out ones faith regarding that which has been prayed about by making the right preparations to receive your blessing. Well in this chapter I want to share with you the importance of making sure that your preparations are in alignment with that which is acted on and ones motives for doing such things.

Our motives for success can sometimes cover a blackboard if we were to write all of them out. But we must examine ourselves at times by asking the questions do my personal motives concerning that which I portray please God? Or am I fooling myself by thinking that my everyday actions are pleasing and acceptable unto God?

Scripture tells us in Matthew 6:33 to seek first the Kingdom of God and all His righteousness and all other things will be added. Proverbs 19:21 says that many are the plans in a man's heart, but it is the Lord's purpose that prevails. What can we learn from these two scriptures concerning this chapter.

Our motives for success can be measured by the weight of these two scriptures, first when we take inventory of our lifestyles, is it a lifestyle that is pleasing to God? Do we sincerely seek God's face to grow closer to Him or to get closer to what God has? When we seek God we need to understand that God wants us to become walking images of His likeness just as Christ was. He wants us to shine forth as a spiritual light into this dark world to be examples of who He is in love, joy, peace, wisdom, faith, patience, self— control, kindness & gentleness which are all the true character traits of our father in Heaven that we saw in the person of Jesus Christ. Now as Christians we need to allow the Spirit of God to help bring about these traits in our lives. For the more we are conformed to the image of Christ, the more we show ourselves approved unto God. Seeking Him earnestly brings His blessing.

When God sees these changes occur in our lives. His purpose for us, as His children, is being reached as we continue to allow Jesus to manifest in us.

The Word of God tells us in Psalms 24:1 that the earth is the Lords and the fullness thereof So we know that everything on this planet including ourselves belong to God. This scripture reminds us that He owns everything and therefore can give to us as abundantly as He desires. What we must grasp is that God not only wants us to be blessed but He wants us to be transformed even the more. Let me explain.

God knows our desires and the motives behind them whether they're right or wrong. Most of us, if we would be honest about it, at one time or another have had ulterior motives concerning things we wanted even from God. But I would have you to know that God was fully aware of our intentions as we in all truth sought His hands (what He could give) instead of His face (who He is). Yet God was not angered by this and even allowed us to go through our problems to bring about a change in our lives that would show how He has molded us into His desired image.

God wants us to be obedient and willing for the right reasons. Sometimes we are showing a mock — form of willingness and obedience in hopes of pleasing God to the point of answering our prayers.

But God knows already when we are sincere or just playing the part. So what does God do to ensure a true spirit of worship? By requiring us not only to be willing and obedient, but to be diligent in them. God tries us and proves our worth not by the trials we face but how we go thru them.

Scripture says that many are the afflictions of the righteous but that God brings us thru everyone of them. (1) Bringing one thru a dilemma brings about the growth of the fruits of the spirit, (2) in a persons life and these fruit can not be developed without time. God is basically telling us it takes a measure of time to receive some of the answers needed to our prayers. He has designed it this way to build within us perseverence, character, and trust.

As these points are developed in us over a period of time, the selfish motives are changed due to the continued development of our relationship with God as we seek to please Him, in truth.

What I love the most about this method is that it always brings about the true purpose that God desires to grow in every man. The shared quest to want to do what Jesus did. Bring glory to the Father and to increase the Kingdom. If you want to learn more in detail about the purpose of the Christian, I would direct you to your local library or bookstore where you'll find the works of some of our modern day great men of God such as T.D. Jakes', "So you call yourself a man, and Woman thou art loosed," Creflo

Dollars' "The Image of Righteousness," and Rick Warren' "The Purpose Driven Life." These are but a few of such writings inspired by God through these men to help us all understand the plan of God for our lives. If you search, you'll find many others.

In Hebrews 6:12 we are told to not become lazy, but to imitate those who through faith and patience inherit what has been promised. Let us take inventory to make sure that our motives do indeed line up with those of the past who learned through much affliction that true happiness, wealth, and prosperity are in Christ Jesus. So let's make sure our hearts are rich towards God, not just the things He has. Then we will be able to sing with the psalmist, "Let the words of my mouth and the meditations of my heart be acceptable in thy sight oh Lord my Rock and my redeemer.(3)

Now lets' meditate on Lesson number 9. As we seek God's favor, let us make sure that our actions are aligned with our true hearts desire. By making sure our motives are not selfish and greedy, but selfless and willing to please God and help bring about the purpose He has placed before us all as Christians.

Lesson 10
Let it Flow

There are several scriptures that will help us to grasp the importance of the meaning of the title of this chapter. When these three words are visually seen, it brings up a mental image of something being released and allowed to come forth freely and unhindered. Imagine a lock and dam water system being opened and millions of gallons of water released to flow unhindered. What an awesome sight! Well in this chapter we're going to learn the importance of storing up and then letting flow the word of God that He has given us concerning our situation.

Now we have established that God can and will speak to us concerning whatever troubles we have. He will give us instruction through the word and as we in faith apply the word given, we will begin to see signs of progress even as the word of God makes the necessary changes in us as he prepares us through willing and obedient lifestyles that have been molded by the afflictions of this world.

Now that our faith, confidence, and trust in God is firmly founded, we can now begin the process of speaking our blessing into existence. Notice that I said begin to speak it into existence with much emphasis on the word begin.

You see many times we will talk about our word God has given. We will even openly say what God has said about our problem. But we need to understand completely what to say, how to say it, and to whom to say it to.

Let's look at a very powerful scripture in Mark 11:23. It says, "I tell you the truth, if anyone says to this mountain 'Go, throw yourself into the sea', and does not doubt in his heart but believes that what he says will happen, it will be done for him." This scripture teaches us the basic fundamentals of speaking things into existence. Now let's dissect this verse to get a better understanding of what Jesus was instructing us in regards to bringing things to pass by our spoken word.

First we need to know what to say. The scripture says speak or say to the mountain, but we must understand that you just can't say anything to your situation (mountain). Your words have to line up with what God says in His Word concerning your situation.

Remember, there is no new thing under the sun. (1) Therefore there are no new problems or issues that are not already addressed in God's word. If you've got a problem, God has an answer. We need to search the scriptures and find out what God is saying, about the situation.

The reason this is important is shown in the books of Isaiah 55:10 – 11 and Jeremiah 1:4 – 12. In Isaiah we see that God's word goes out and does not return unto Him void, but will accomplish what He desires and achieve the purpose for which it was sent. Notice that "His word" accomplishes and achieves the purposes sent for. His word will get the job done. In Jeremiah God tells a young Jeremiah not to say what he himself thinks, but what God tells him to say.

God tells Jeremiah that he most say all that he has been told and to not be afraid. Why, because God tells this young individual who is seemingly unsure of himself that as he speaks the words that God has given him to say with confidence, God will watch over His word to perform it. In other words, as we say what God says about the situation in faith not doubting, God will make sure those same words will come to pass because those are His words coming out of your mouth.

Second we need to know how to say it. This point revolves around the importance of speaking your God giving word with confidence, and authority. You have got to wholeheartedly believe the word God has given you to speak about, or over your situation as absolute truth, and that there is no other solution other than what God has said. We previously discussed in chapter 4 the importance of taking God at His word to ensure success, deliverance, and victory in our lives. But you must be confident in the Word.

We also must speak His word with authority. In the armed forces we have different ranks that signify the different levels of authority given to order command. A private can not give orders of instruction to a General because he does not have the authority to do so, whereas that same General can not only give orders to that private but has the authority to give command over several brigades which includes thousands of soldiers.

Well Christ has given us authority in His word. In Luke 10:19 Jesus told those He had chosen," I have given you authority (power) to trample on snakes and scorpions and to overcome all the power of the enemy.

In knowing this truth, we can now speak our God given word of instruction with assurance that God himself has given us the right to say to our situation what will cause it to disappear. His word, because of the God given authority you have, has now become your word in Christ Jesus. Hallelujah!

Third, exactly to whom are we saying all these authorized power filled words of faith to? Are we talking to God, telling Him to move the problem? No. Remember God is not the problem nor did He cause it. He has given us the authority to speak His word too, so He's not going to do what He's enable us to do.

Do we speak to the devil commanding him to go and remove the problem? No. Even though be may be a major reason the problem exists, the situation is not beholden to him, but to the one who has the authority. Guess who that is?

We must speak and say the words that we have received from God in the power of His given authority, directly to our situation. The scripture in Mark 11:23 tells us to say to the mountain. So we need to speak to our problem the word God has given us to say in all confidence and with all the authority He has given us. Know that His word in our mouth will accomplish the task set before it.

Why, because God watches over His word that He has given us to say to make sure it performs all that it speaks of. This is what God says He will do.

I was told once that even a continous droppings of water can create a gorge in a granite floor given enough time. The Grand Canyon was even formed by a steady flow of water. God's word coming out of your mouth will in time bring about a major change regarding whatever your situation brings. The key is to keep the words flowing.

Don't tire of saying what God has given you to say even though you don't see immediate results. Remember Rome wasn't built in a day and neither was the Grand Canyon.

Now let's meditate on Lessen number 10. Begin to let God's words flow out of your mouth in confidence and power, knowing that His word in your mouth has authoritative power and God watches over it to bring it to pass. So let the words flow in faith and patience for you will receive if you don't give up.

Lesson 11
Hold the load

We have talked about in full the process of seed, time, and harvest. We have gone over how prayer, & preparation will bring about God's provision. So now there is but one topic left for us to address. How to hold the load.

The load represents your blessing. Some also refer to this as the breakthrough. But however you describe it the bottom line is that it represents the crossing of the finish line, the winning of the prize, the reaping of the harvest, or the manifestation of your miracle.

This is the time you've been waiting for. You have arrived at your sought after destination. Your season is here, your change has come, and your time is now.

You've remained steadfast in the word, showed Godly character as you diligently walked by faith allowing God to mold you through afflictions, and continued to do that what you believed as God instructed. So after all this, what is left? Well something that I have learned that is essential to holding on to your blessing.

In Ephesians 6:7 — 8 it says that we should serve whole heartedly as if you were serving the Lord, not men because you know that the Lord will reward everyone for whatever good he does, whether he is slave or free. God's blessings rain down on those who are consistent to what He represents. God represents love, hope, and faith. And love is the greatest of all.

Everything that has been discussed from chapter one up to now can only be empowered by the God kind of love. Agape love is the love that gives to the utmost. For God so loved the world that He gave us his only begotten Son, Jesus.(1) Jesus even said that no greater love is there than the love that would cause a man to lay down his life for his friend.(2) As we walk this Christian way we must walk in the fullness of love.

There was a man who once said that the words you profess out of your mouth builds the road over which faith will carry its mighty cargo. When I picture this in my mind, I see a giant heavenly 18— wheeler traveling down this golden road of the confessed words of my mouth, which connects the heavenly realm to the earth realm.

This 18— wheeler represents faith and the fuel that keeps that 18 — wheeler rolling is love. Why, because faith is activated by love. So if you haven't been living in and by the spirit of love, you are going to have a long wait ahead of you before your breakthrough comes. So make sure your faith truck is filled with the fuel of love because you wouldn't want to loose out on that what you've been hoping for due to a lack of love! Remember love truly is the key that opens the door to your faith filled miracle.

So let us remember to not become weary in our love — based well doing, for we know that in due time we will receive our reward if we don't give up. And with every opportunity, let us do good to all men, especially those of the house hold of faith.(3) This is a required act of love that must be kept constant before, during, and even after our blessing.

God desires to give all to us according to His promised word, but in order to insure our harvest let us remember to love in all our actions for this is the will of God for us! Then we will be able to "Hold the Load."

Now let's meditate on lesson number 11. As we walk out all of that which we have learned regarding prayer, preparation, and provision let us hold fast to our charge to continuously walk in love even as stated in Hebrews 6:10. Our love in faith will help us to hold the load and keep it as well.

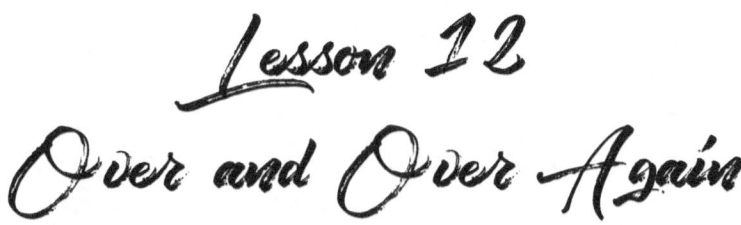

Lesson 12
Over and Over Again

We have now reached the end of our little, yet informative lessons that are designed to stir us up, and steer us in the right direction when we are in need of relief, victory and deliverance in whatever adversity may arise.

In this final chapter I want to stress the importance of putting into practice all that we have learned in order to ensure success. We as Christians must strive to maintain a consistency in our walk in every area of our lives. This is especially true in regards to all that we have discussed thus far.

God is not only looking for willingness and obedience in us but also consistent behavior in all that we do. Especially in our prayer life. God wants to talk to us daily and desires for an open relationship that is growing and productive.

I can recall how my father would go through all the required steps to develop, plant, and nurture to full maturity all the fruits and vegetables that were planted in the garden.

I remember, what caused these moments to be forever locked inside my mind. These were two truths that I must share at this time.

First, hands on training. My dad would explain to me things that I would see him do in the garden such as shoring up the rows by pulling the loose soil up to the top of the rows and around the sprouting plants. Then he would do his best to peak my interest by telling of what nice produce we would have if we took extra good care of the sprouts. By then I was eager enough to try my hand at shoring up the rows, with little success I might add, but my dad continued to lovingly encourage me on. Even though I could plainly see that my work was a weak example of his.

Yet he continued to urge me on, and because of the special attention given me even while realizing my work wasn't even comparable to anything that he had done, I was encouraged to continue to try. Please keep this in mind when you begin to put these lessons into effect. You're probably not going to get everything exactly right, but do not let this discourage you, just remember that the race is not to the swift or the battle to the strong,.....but time and chance happen to them all.(1)

If we stay diligent every work will be rewarded in time, for that what we sow must sooner or later be reaped. Everything will change. Don't stop trying until you get it right. Remember that you will reap if you don't give up. The woman who sought relief at the hands of the un —just judge was finally rewarded because of her diligence.(2) What about you?

Second, the purpose of reinforcement. Every year we would plant a spring and early fall garden. For as far back as I can remember up until my father became ill and died of cancer.

Over those years that he planted and worked those gardens, his methods never changed or `process was altered. And with each planting, whether spring or fall, he would urge me to put into practice all that I had learned. Granted, many times he had to re – instruct me regarding certain points, but once corrected I was back at it again. As I got older and stronger my confidence grew as well and I could do everything required with skill to bring about the end results of a successful garden, produce!

Once you've gone thru this book you may have to refer back to certain chapters to remind you of certain points. But the key is to continue to practice all these lessons regularly until you've got it down solid.

God desires for everyone of us to be blessed and at peace. But we must continue to apply that what we have learned. Remember what the Lord Jesus taught us in Luke 8:15, "But the seed on good soil stands for those with a noble and good heart, who hear the word, retain it, and by persevering produce a crop.

So let's all join in and press for success in our prayer life with true endurance knowing that God's word never fails, and His instructions will bring about the results He has promised. Yes weeping may endure for a night but joy comes in the morning.(3) Trust God my fellow Christian for your problem has indeed "come to pass." For everything has a season. So stay prayed up, get prepared and wait for the provision.

Let's meditate on Lesson number 12. Practice these 12 lessons in a diligent and consistent manner to ensure God 's best results from your harvest.

Scriptural Reference

Chapter One
1. Jeremiah 4:3 and Hosea 10:12 2. Acts 2:14 – 47 3. Luke 8:4 – 15

Chapter Two
1. Luke 8:11 2. John 5:14 – 15 3. Hebrews 11:6 4. Jeremiah 1:12 5. Isaiah 55:11 6. Psalms 138:2 7. St. John 6:63

Chapter Three
1. Numbers 23:19

Chapter Four
1. Isaiah 55:8 – 9 2. St. John 14:15

Chapter Five
1. Psalms 119:68 2. James 1:17

Chapter Six
1. 2nd Corinthians 4:13 2. 2nd Corinthians 5:7 3. Romans 4:17

Chapter Seven
1. Ist Timothy 1:7 2. Numbers 14:26 – 43

Chapter Eight (No References)

Chapter Nine
1. Psalms 34:19 2. Galatians 5:22 – 23 3. Psalms 19:14

Chapter Ten
1. Ecclesiastes 1:9

Chapter Eleven
1. St. John 3:16 2. St. John 15:13 3. Galatians 6:9 – 10

Chapter Twelve
1. Ecclesiastes 9:11 2. Luke 18:1 – 8 3. Psalms 30:5

Appendix

Prayers of Support for each lesson.

Chapter One — (prayer located at the end of the chapter.)

Chapter two — Father in Heaven, we come to you seeking your provision for my problem that is given within your word. Father I have learned that every situation I face in life is answered within your word, therefore guide me with the power of your Holy Spirit to scriptures and verses that will enlighten me regarding my problem in Jesus name, Amen.

Chapter Three — Father in Heaven, I come to you seeking a more intimate relationship with You. I want to please you Lord as a true worshiper in spirit and truth. Help my growth in confidence to know your voice above all others so I may be led by your word of truth in facing my problem. Father I know your word is above all and is final in all areas. Help me to clearly hear and distinguish your instructions in Jesus' name, Amen.

Chapter Four — Father in Heaven, help me to faithfully follow your instructions to the letter. I trust you Lord and my heart in confident in your word of deliverance. And if the words of instruction seem odd or strange, strengthen me Lord in faith to not think my way out of my blessing by allowing doubt to seep in while trying to figure things out in Jesus' name, Amen.

Chapter Five — Father in Heaven, help me to understand that even though I don't see anything happening yet concerning my problem, You are still at work regarding my requests and through the word you have given me as instruction help me to lean on it as well as a constant reminder that you have not forgotten me in Jesus' name, Amen.

Chapter Six — Father in Heaven, help me to lock in on your word by meditating on that what you've spoken to me both night and day. Give me the discipline to enact my imagination to see your word at work on my behalf that I may not grow weary and loose focus on your promise to me in Jesus' name, Amen.

Chapter Seven — Father in Heaven, help me to be patient as your Word renews my mind and allows me the wisdom to recognize the subtle changes brought about by your work in my life and my situation. I know by faith that with each passing day I grow stronger in your Word and I have confidence that even now you are preparing me to be able to recognize signs of progress made by you. In Jesus' name, Amen.

Chapter Eight — Father in Heaven help me to ignite my faith in making preparations for all that you have promised to me in accordance to Your word of instruction in Jesus' name, Amen.

Chapter Nine — Father in Heaven I have a sincerely concern about my motives and desires. I want to truly line up with Your will for my life even with regards to my needs and requested relief Lord show me my heart and if there is anything within me that does not bring glory to You, forgive me and please help to remove it completely that nothing may hinder my growth in Your grace and mercy in Jesus name, Amen.

"Chapter Ten - Father in Heaven we thank you even now for the word of instruction that you have given concerning my situation. Now Lord help me to allow that word of faith to flow from me with power, confidence and consistency needed to bring about my change in Jesus' name, Amen.

Chapter Eleven - I thank you Father in Heaven for your agape love that you have planted into my heart. I thank you for teaching me to nourish it with Your word and to allow it to come forth as one of my developed fruits of the spirit. Help me Lord to continuously walk in the fullness of this love towards all people in Jesus' name, Amen.

Chapter Twelve - Father in Heaven help me to put all that I've learned in this book to practice in a consistent manner. Allow me to see when I'm not following the process and help me to get back on the right path in Jesus' name, Amen."

www.ingramcontent.com/pod-product-compliance
Lightning Source LLC
Chambersburg PA
CBHW031229120626
46545CB00003B/1048